Inner Child:

Healing From Within

Moonsoulchild

ISBN: 9798359344784

This collection is all about healing my inner child. It's opening up old wounds. It's freeing myself from fears, secrets, and suppressed memories. To heal is to do the hard work… it's facing every hurtful emotion… it's shutting down past feelings when they try to explode through random moments in my life. I am focused on my current path. I am in touch with my mind, body, and soul. My heart is pure. I only hold the best intentions. Discovering myself through the years has been a painful yet bittersweet process. The first step is confronting and forgiving. I'm standing in my truth and this time I won't run from it. Be aware this collection can trigger some, but this is my story… I'm only telling it in the best way I know how to express it.

A letter to my Inner Child

You don't need to apologize for neglecting me at the times I reached out to console you, I understand you were grieving a version of yourself you weren't familiar with. I wasn't going to let you drown in your own self-destruction but I tried to comfort you many times through memories and things that could remind you of your gift but you stayed stuck in your ways and I don't blame you for trying to live without me but it was me who wiped those silent tears while you broke every time you overextended your heart to those who weren't worthy. I pondered many times, did you forget me? it was like you disguised yourself, a façade only I wasn't fooled by. You were living a life with the only truth told was your desire to show your heart. Without a doubt, you succeeded but always got stuck in the intangible of not being loved in return. I tried to guide you through the dark. I thought my years of knowledge could heal you, but you never listened. It was important for you to learn your lesson and you did but through so much heartbreak. You grew stronger and wiser, I'm so proud of you.

Write a letter to your inner-child

Heart to Hearts with my Inner child

I promised you I would never dig up what I made peace with, that once I healed from it I wouldn't let it harass me into being an afterthought. I knew the cost of dredging up the delicate moments but reflecting was better than suppressing. I know you felt like revisiting those broken moments would only revive those fires that couldn't be tamed. I know you felt I would sink back into that dark place. I know parts of you still live there. I want you to know I'm sorry, for dragging you through the misery like a bad song on repeat. I want you to know, that I always heard you, I just wasn't ready to listen. I want to apologize for neglecting you while I searched for ways to free myself, I should have catered to you, too. I ran from you instead of embracing you. I thought the trauma that surrounded my heart was me surviving my karma. I should have trusted you.

Heart to Heart with your Inner Child

Inner Child Affirmations:

I am worthy.
I am worthy of love.
I am worthy of happiness.
I am worthy of peace.
I am worthy of balance.

I can survive any storm.
I can fight with strength.
I can win with love.
I can overcome any battle.

I give myself patience.
I give myself grace.

I honor the soul I've become.

Inner Child Affirmations:

Meet my insecurities…

I was insecure about my teeth growing up, having a huge gap (which seemed out of the norm) so, I felt it defined me in the worst way. I felt fitting in seemed more welcoming. Having a gap was only one thing, but being skinny was another thing everyone highlighted when it came to me. Everyone defining my size every time they saw me led me to an unhealthy relationship with my body. I never felt comfortable in my skin. Acne so became fluent in high school. I was the quiet girl who was "so skinny" with a gap that always broke out. I tried so hard to run from being the girl who stood out because it seemed to always make me uncomfortable. I hated being the center of any universe. I was introverted. I never hurt a soul… I never understood why I deserved to be treated like I wasn't worthy because of every physical feature. *No one took the time to understand me.*

What are your insecurities?

Your insecurities are more prominent
In your mind,
than they are to a stranger's eyes

...remember that.

You were lost.

You were stuck in your insecurities… which burned you a lot of the time. You never saw the beauty in you, so you searched for beauty in everyone else but couldn't come to terms with giving the same love to yourself. You broke your heart many times.

I limited the impact my insecurities hold over me. I keep people who inspire me around me and detach myself from anyone who tries to drown me. I'm where I need to be... but I'm only growing from here.

I love the view.

Opinions have become my insecurities… they live inside me—they never truly disappear. Fighting insecurities is like fighting a battle you'll never win, how you see yourself is always a reflection of those opinions. I fought to win, to overcome every bad thing I heard. I didn't realize every opinion was a reflection of their insecurities. I always wished I could see myself through someone else's eyes… maybe then I could have loved myself more. I fought for so long to understand what made me beautiful.

Don't let someone's insecurities blind you
into believing they're yours too. Don't let
society trap you into believing a size 0 is the
look. It doesn't define your beauty.
Be healthy. Be happy. Love all of you.

Physical beauty fades
your soul never will.

Growing up my gap was a lot bigger because my teeth were growing in and fitting into place… people found it as a way to bully me or make me feel less attractive… but as I grew up it became something that tied into what made me unique. I couldn't picture myself without it. I met people who admired it about me—and some not so much. The thing most important was how I felt about it… I've grown to love it. I go through the motions and relive those moments of people using it as a weapon against me. I don't blame them… with the insecurities they hold within themselves it's hard to see someone confident. I reached a place in my life where people's words don't hurt me, especially when it's something I defeated. No one can make me feel insecure about something I lived and overcame. I stressed about being accepted for these flaws—it's my soul that matters. *I don't want anyone who praises perfection around me.*

Mirror Talks

I don't recognize you
through acne, blemishes
and scars
your thin frame
with an ass out of place
a gap too big, afraid to speak

Things I often highlighted
Things I resented
when I looked in the mirror
there was no trace of you
just the noise of everyone around you
"do you eat"
"nice ass"
"I only date a woman with clear skin"

I was a teenager with hormones raging
an identity crisis
I don't know why I was chosen
I don't know why it was me

The stigma forever lies within me
I don't think I'll ever find me
Or love me…

What if no one else does?

Have a "Mirror Talk"

What I wish I could have told my inner child…

Don't be so hard on yourself… be a kid. Don't put so much pressure on fitting it, there was a reason you were meant to stand out. The projections of others are their insecurities… don't let them define how you love yourself. Love who loves you, don't try and work overtime trying to find love in those who left you… those who can't see how amazing you are. These moments of your life are for having fun, learning, and being free. Wait to grow up… enjoy your youth.

What I wish I could have told my inner child...

To my father…

Till this day I don't know why you walked away, I get the run around every time I try to circle back around … you always leave me without a clue. I found stuff through my sources, which could have been the reason, and it hurt like hell. I wanted the truth until it was too heavy. Your demons took control of you and you chose to leave us… I couldn't understand that then, but I get it now. I was a child then, it wasn't fair growing up with you one minute… loving me and being present to being a ghost. I'm guessing there wasn't a reason that sounded good enough for you to give, maybe you didn't think I could hold something that heavy… I wish you could have trusted me. I wish I didn't have to live without you for ten years of my life… wondering what you're doing out there in the world if you're okay… if you loved me.

I developed those same patterns—ghosting when it was time to walk away. I was selfish and chose no words because hurting someone I loved would only hurt me, so I chose to let them suffer without involving me. I don't think that's something to be proud to take with me through life… not know how to communicate because I developed a comfort with myself. Isolation and loneliness are a mix of peace for me. I was dragging myself through hell—I didn't know myself at all. You missed some of the biggest moments of my life. You never called. Till this day, you're here but you're still distant. Sometimes I wonder, *what's the point if when I'm in the same room with you and you feel like a complete stranger…*

I was surrounded by so much love
until it came to the love
I was deprived of
I felt unworthy.
How powerful your absence was
To deprive me of
The love I needed

- *I needed you*

My safe place as a kid was being around anyone I felt safe with… it wasn't a particular place, it was certain people. I closed myself off to everyone… it was rare when I opened myself up to anyone, so when I did, it was a safe space for me. I think that's why it always hurt so much when someone of those same people betrayed me, left me, and ghosted me. I thought allowing them in would mean they would never go. Opening myself up to trust anyone was hard enough.

I wish my inner child knew the difference between love and when it's time to go, that everyone wasn't a safe place… and some will only be safe for the moment. So, not fully invest myself deeply in anyone because of how fleeting it can be.

At 29, my safe place is still attached to certain individuals but it's on a different frequency. I don't allow everyone in and I don't allow anyone to take with them. I found solace in my solitude—I don't need a soul to keep me happy or to make me happy. I can sit with myself and enjoy my own company without the feeling of loneliness creeping up. I think that's one of the painful lessons I learned in my journey, to not invest everything I have into one particular person or thing, because when it's over, all of me goes with them and I end up broken.

One thing I wish I could have told my inner child when it came to investing energy into anything:

Don't give all of yourself, it will only break you when it ends. Nothing lasts forever—forever is something that we create in our minds to believe we can outlive our time here on earth. We're all going to expire... so live like no one is watching but know that everything you put into every connection might not be reciprocated. Everything you invest in might not be a good investment. Sometimes love feels good at the moment but you realize it was lust and you were confused. Sometimes things end and you discover something more incredible. Sometimes things last a lifetime. I wish I could have told you not to put all of you into everything you've ever wanted. *I wish I could have told you to save some for yourself.*

What was your "safe place" as a kid?

To my inner child

Searching for your safe place opens the door for comfort in ways that aren't for you… or ways that aren't healthy for you. You accept them because you want to feel something. Someone being your safe place is more than feeling love, it's someone who doesn't make you question their intentions or love. it's someone who is honest and doesn't lie to you. it's someone who never makes you number two. You deserve a safe space to share your love with… someone with who you find a home, but before you find them… I hope you set a new foundation, the right boundaries, and build yourself a home that can't be taken from you—one without the sadness attached. This time you won't allow strangers to create a safe place out of your bond with trauma.

Over the years I created my safe place in souls who were trauma-bonded like me, to feel familiar… maybe even help them heal so I could forget about my suffering. Being the savior made me feel superior. It made me feel needed, something I never felt. My trauma sunk me deeper into this cycle of self-destruction when I couldn't save anyone and they ended up being a threat to my heart. Trauma bonded us but it left us empty and not empowered. It left us even more broken. I felt safe surrounded by those who were struggling to fight their demons because I could find myself in them—alone and afraid but somehow I felt smaller.

My safe place today is surrounded by love, bliss, and reciprocation in the form of peace. I only keep souls around me who aren't damaged by my healing. I've unlearned the patterns of being the savior and learned the biggest lessons… no one can be healed unless they put in the work themselves. I had to stop finding myself in others because it was an excuse to feel smaller, to hide from my trauma. I surround myself with people who adore me more, who listen and inspire me to be my own, and who appreciate who I am at the core of my being. I surround myself in spaces that don't compete, compare, or dimmish my ability to love. I don't surround myself with anyone who makes me feel hard to love.

Explain your "safe place" today:

Codependent

I felt safe with you
until you left,
then I feared
loneliness
abandonment
and never being good enough.
I thought love
would keep us entangled forever

...that investment cost me so much

No Love Found

You were my **safe place**
my *go-to,*
the only one I'd run to.
Until
you shattered me,
leaving me blue.
Taking all of me
piece by piece, with you

…why was it so easy for you?

Fear and rejection –
one hell of a mix
 a rush of shame,
 a shadow of doubt
 a moment of weakness
 a voice for the demons.
It festered, thrived
It became a monster

...one I couldn't hide

Thoughts from the past

Nothing in life seemed real. I was always chasing love--and to be loved. I was always trying to find someone who can make me feel different instead of taking my heart for a joy ride with no intention to love me. Nothing good ever stuck—it was always fleeting. I couldn't hold it for long… I couldn't savor the feeling. The love I received from those I needed wasn't always reciprocated. Everyone who promised forever only meant until they found better. I don't know how I had faith behind the shadow. I became naive, small-minded, and bitter. I was the cause of my heart's demise. There was no greater loss than hindering my growth and the fear of who I'd become. I never gave the best love to myself… I was too busy saving that for everyone else.

Write out feelings from your past

Unworthiness –
a feeling I could never suppress
I couldn't escape or attest
It settled, became established
it made a home in me.
It's the scar I wear everywhere, every day

This isn't what I asked for
when I said **I wanted forever**…

To be free

The word "childlike" to me is to be free. Free of everything that once held me hostage. To be a kid again… to live the life that came easy once until it became tainted by insecurities, loss, and identity theft. To be free in the sense of having no problems within, before things got heavy. Trauma healed without having me in a constant chokehold. My inner child cries every time I fall back into old patterns of self-sabotage and self-doubt. Memories I wish to forget but use to reflect on when I needed a reminder to not fall into the same toxic cycle. To be free… that's all I ever wanted.

What does childlike mean to you?

I'm a natural nurturer. It came to me at a young age. Being surrounded by so much love was something that I adapted to… to take care of everyone I love and to shower them with everything they need. I realize now that may have been too much when it came to a lot of situations with people throughout my life. I also became a healer, believing I could save anyone from the pain they were going through. I didn't want anyone to suffer—I wanted to protect them and their heart at all costs. I should have given them enough room to breathe. I should have been a listening ear… a shoulder to cry on. I shouldn't have been the thing they depended on, knowing I couldn't give them everything they needed.

What role do you play in your life?

I dreamt of being everything as a kid. It always came back to help others in some way. I wanted others to be included because I felt my purpose was bigger than just myself. I felt most fulfilled when I helped someone. I wanted to be a teacher. I wanted to be a vet. I wanted to be a therapist. I admired the ability to make others feel something other than loneliness, heartbreak, and sadness. To help someone find their way to healing… to be an inspiration along the way.

Writing chose me. Being an author is a dream, but it wasn't in the beginning. I fell in love with expressing my emotions and freeing myself of everything that kept me from every dream. I was here to heal, inspire, and love. this is the real dream. **I'm living it.**

What did you dream to be?

When I was young I was most proud when I accomplished something I loved to do but got confirmation from others that I was good. I was very shy growing up so I didn't have the confidence when it came to doing anything publicly, but I enjoyed dance because at the time it was something I was interested in… I performed on a stage more than once. I was terrified – the bright lights and the huge crowd. the best advice I ever got was to act like I was the only one at that moment… that no one was watching. I felt free every time I did something outside my comfort zone… I felt so proud to succeed in something I thought I'd fail at.

What made you proud as a kid?

Everyone knew me as the quiet girl, the one who never talked. I had a few friends and that's what mattered most to me. I struggled in school. I struggled to focus. I struggled to get the work done successfully—especially when it came to stuff I wasn't interested in. I had a hard time comprehending… I was diagnosed with a reading comprehension disorder. I was able to get extra time on my tests (because when it came to them my anxious nerves took over). I was put into classes that a lot of the kids in my grade weren't in… but the friends I found in those classes were some of my best friends. This disorder was strong until I went to high school and I was able to take college courses without the extra help. I struggled a lot because I wasn't the biggest fan of school, looking back at it now… I'm creative, I love to create… book smart wasn't my intelligence. To think I became a writer—an author after going through my life with this disorder. Some may think I couldn't have done it. Yes, maybe my grammar isn't perfect. Maybe I make a lot of mistakes. If you knew what it felt like to live most of my life the way I felt... you'd understand how amazing it feels to conquer everything it took for me to become the person I am today. I went to college. I got a certificate for medical admin assistant. It all came back to writing. I'm doing the best I can. I'm so proud of who I am and who I've become. I never discredit the journey. Every piece of who I was is a part of who I am today.

When did you first realize that you were different from other children?

Going into high school I felt I was no longer a child. I felt like I was walking into a whole new world. I was learning things about myself. I was growing. I didn't know I was still a child. I was someone who thought high school was your time to "have it figured out" and after you leave you to start your life out the way you planned. If I'm being honest, I don't think I became an adult until I was twenty-five. I made a lot of dumb decisions in my 20s, probably more than I did in my teenage years. I realize now my 20s were my learning years—the era of making mistakes and discovering myself little by little through all the heartache, loss, and every moment. I thought I'd have a child by twenty-five. I thought I'd find love early… as I always wished for. I was chasing the dream and not the reality. My maturity was always there, but not in the way when I turned twenty-five. That was the year of my ultimate change—for the bad and the good. Life has been amazing since, with the ups and downs. I will never resent the journey. I'm so blessed to have learned the lessons I did… it made me into this beautiful soul.

When did you feel as though you were no longer a "child"?

I always felt like I was the kid who wanted so badly to grow up. I never tried acting older than I was… it was just more that I couldn't wait to grow up and be an adult. To have my own home. To have my own family. To have my own money to buy what I want. I grew up fortunate, there was always food on the table and a roof over our heads. I grew up thankful. We were far from rich, but my childhood wasn't poor. I was always thankful for what I received, I never asked for much. I was happy regardless. We didn't always get new school clothes so I was made fun of a lot for having the same clothes as the years before. We didn't get to eat out often. We ate what my mom could afford. My mom was a single mother, we lived with my grandparents so they helped raise us when she worked two jobs to provide. I'm thankful for living how we did even if some may say it wasn't the best living arrangement. Our house was old but it held some of the greatest memories—some of the saddest too. The traumatic experiences in my life could have changed me for the worst… I may have suppressed some emotions that held a lot of heartaches but the good always outweighed the bad at that exact moment.

Today, I wished I could have stayed a kid. I wish I didn't rush to grow up. I enjoyed my childhood when it came to playing creative games outdoors and not coming in until it was dark. Not having a job to work eight or more hours at just to come home eat and sleep for the next day. As a kid, we always highlight the things we don't have when we compare them to others who do have, and we rush to grow up… without realizing how free it was to be a child. Being an adult is a constant worry and a lot of bills. It makes me appreciate those who raised me more. I know it's not easy, but the dedication and love to always make sure we were good… I'll always take that with me.

Were you in a rush to grow up or did you want to stay a child forever?

As a kid, I always idolized those who were good to me—and those who inspired me. Sometimes it was a close family member... sometimes it was someone who I wanted to be when I grew up. Who I wanted to be always changed as I changed through the years but my mentors always stayed the same. There wasn't a lot but certain teachers will always remember to this day when it comes to pushing me and making me reach my full potential. those who believed in me when I couldn't hold the confidence myself. I met a lot of people throughout my journey and they will always hold space in my heart. I will always take those memories with me and spread the same love and inspiration to everyone. those certain connections meant a lot to me because I did not open up to everyone, so when I felt it was safe I let my guard down and they became a safe place. they never let me down. That was when I started to break out of my shell—the one I hid most of myself in my whole life.

Who did you idolize or admire as a child?

I'm grateful for the laughter
for the meals
for the home I resided,
the friends I made.
I'm grateful for the lows
the losses
that turned into lessons
I'm grateful for
the blessings that kept on giving.

I'm grateful to be healthy
to be alive
to be breathing

...I'm so grateful to be me

Write things from your childhood that you're grateful for:

Forgiveness –

I don't seek it
I don't chase it
It doesn't live within closure.
The trauma won't fade
My heart will still ache.
Forgiveness isn't treasure
It's not a healing stone.

I could heal on my own
I didn't need their apologies
Their guilt and lies

To those who wronged me,
I forgive you –
for me,
for the sake of being free of you

forgiveness is reserved
for those
who deserve a second chance
not for those who abuse them

What does forgiveness mean to you?

I believe I'm worthy of forgiveness
if I've ever wronged you,
I didn't just apologize…
I took accountability for my projections.
I never held grudges
and I never had ill intentions.
I won't ask for forgiveness,
I'm okay living with my decisions
my lessons.
I need to grace myself
with forgiveness,
to heal, to grow.

What's the #1 reason you are deserving of self-forgiveness?

Self-sabotage—
I would, every time I felt unworthy
I built up this idea of me
that became crushed
every time I saw the real me.
I couldn't see my beauty.
I masked myself for everyone,
when I looked in the mirror
I only saw the one
who would never be worthy

Have you induldged in self-sabatoage?

Projections—
I never meant to burden anyone with them
I never wanted to break anyone
I just wanted to be loved.
The trauma I didn't heal from
made me so hard to love.
I was blaming everyone
for my heartache.
It was my projections that broke everyone
It was my trauma
that continued to destroy me.

...I'm sorry

What are your projections?

Repetitive Patterns

Loving people who never loved me back and trying to save everyone from their trauma. I hated seeing anyone in pain. I wanted to be loved. I thought if I could help someone heal, maybe they would love me too. I didn't know at the time that's not how love bloomed. I developed codependency traits when I suppressed myself to their ways. I felt purpose when I could help save and free them of the emotional trauma… without knowing they only suppressed the feeling and ended up hurting me more in the end. I was left to pick up more pieces. I was left with nothing. This toxic cycle became my life for years until I learned to detach myself from being the savior… to not try and attach love to everyone because it never brought me the one. It only left me to be the broken one.

What are some of your repetitive patterns?

How do you think people see you?

Is there a pattern in the way you judge others?
Is there a pattern in how you judge yourself?

What's the biggest misconception people have about you?

Which emotion tends to get you into trouble most often?

What stories about yourself do you replay most often?

There's no single memory that holds significance, but multiple. Remembering my younger years makes me remember the time I was close to my family—the parties, random get-togethers… just the closeness I had with some of them, those memories hold so much happiness in my heart. Remembering the times when my grandparents were still here, not only in spirit. Remembering a certain smell. A memory attached to a song. Those memories are still so vividly living within my soul. I smiled more than I cried. I had wonderful people in my corner raising me and helping me bloom into the beautiful soul I've come to be. My inner child is forever healing. My inner child is also very proud.

Thank you for reading this collection.
I hope you fill in the blanks and get to the source of your healing. Whenever you are right now on your journey, check in with your inner child often… give them love too. As you grow you will leave behind a lot, but never allow yourself to distance yourself from your inner child and your intuition. They're what keep us safe in this world—never neglect them. You do yourself a disservice when you don't give yourself the love and grace you deserve.

All Platforms:

Instagram: Moonsoulchild
Twitter: Bymoonsoulchild
Facebook: Moonsoulchild
Tiktok: Bymoonsoulchild
Apple Music: Moonsoulchild
Spotify: Moonsoulchild

Moonsoulchild.com

Anonymous Stories

(submissions by supports)

Here's to sharing our truth

Anonymous 1:

To me, inner child healing in its simplest definition is giving/showing love to that part of you that feels unloved, unheard, and unseen or loving the version of you that felt unloved for who you are when you were a child or giving yourself the love you wish you were given /shown as a child

As a young girl, growing up I experienced hate, discrimination, and bullying from my peers in school, teachers, and family members, I was also shamed for my imperfections and mistakes, and people projected their insecurities on me by trying what they could to make me feel bad about myself and body. I also didn't feel seen and understood and wasn't given enough attention that I needed as a child by my parents. All these experiences made me a love addict, I was always looking for love outside of myself, so I played small, people pleased, was overgiving, stayed in toxic relationships, was moving from one romantic relationship to another in search of love, chose people's happiness and well-being over mine, wasn't able to set boundaries and also didn't feel good about myself. My inner child didn't want to feel unloved and I was subconsciously looking for love & validation outside myself.

I started my inner child healing journey by writing a love letter to my inner child, letting her know that all that happened wasn't her fault at all and shouldn't blame herself for how unfairly she was treated.

Another practice that helped me heal my inner child was inner child visualization meditation. I visualized my inner child right in front of me while I make her feel loved, in the meditation practice through visualization, I give my inner child everything, all the love and validation she needed, I also asked her what she needs, give her all the things I loved as a child, all I ever wanted as a child, I play with her, have fun with her, treat her like I would treat my daughter. All in the visualization meditation practice.

Other ways I've healed my inner child was to practice self-compassion, honor my childish nature, honor my humanness, letting go of self-criticism, giving myself the grace to be human and imperfect, honoring the things I loved as a child like watching my favorite cartoon when I was younger, feeling my emotions without judgment, by not letting myself to see my inner child as a problem or a part of me that needs fixing but instead seeing my inner child as a part of me that needs my unconditional love, accepting the truth that there's nothing wrong with me regardless and everything about me is divine and perfect. All these have helped me heal my inner child and are still helping me build a healthy and loving relationship with myself.

Anonymous 2:

My childhood was filled with abuse of ALL varieties, and neglect by my mom. As an adult, I thought the people in my life should abide by my triggers and cater to me when I'm upset. But now I see that is just selfish.

No one is obligated to care… the people that did and do, don't have to. I can sit here and be negative and angry all I want, but I'm just gonna lose people, because who wants to be around negativity all the time? Hell, I didn't even wanna be around me sometimes. I wanted to be happy. I was so tired of being angry all the time. I have every reason in the world to be a shitty person… to be negative because nothing in my life ever gave me anything to be genuinely happy about. Survival and anger were all I knew. But as I got older, I had kids and got married, I realized…. I wanna give them the world. I don't ever want to be the villain in their story. I learned how to deal with the trauma and let it go. I have struggled for so long trying to forgive my mom, but recently I learned that I don't have to forgive anyone. Especially my mother. It's okay to just accept what happened and move on. Forgiveness is not required… after I realized that, I don't have that pedestal of anger anymore. I can be alone without losing my mind or my thoughts eating at me. I can move on and thrive within myself so the people around me can enjoy my presence without walking on eggshells. I still have my flaws, and some work to do, but overall life is so much brighter now.

Anonymous 3:

Disappointed. How my life started but I refuse to let it end that way. A daddy-less daddy's girl with no true connection to my mother. So who am I? A being who has experienced countless disappointments in herself and others. A heart full of love yet no one to experience it with. Accepting the poorest of relationships to fill a void, knowing in the end disappointment will be the result. Disappointed. Through life's trials and my circumstances, I grew to live in the comfort of anxiety, hurt, and none other than disappointment. Until one day I decided that disappointment could no longer lead my life and with my newfound hope, happiness lives within me. Happiness is what I allow in my presence. Happiness. Yeah, I like that.

Anonymous 4:

I see you. I see you climbing the branches of the trees around the pond. I see you swimming in the pool pretending to be a mermaid, holding your breath as the second's tick by. I see you when I pass by the swings in the old elementary school playground. I see your joy. However, I see you when you trip and scrape your knee and when you curl into a ball and cry for help. It's okay. Shed those tears because I am here with you. I love you when you laugh, but I love you, even more, when you let yourself feel everything this beautiful world has created for your to experience. I see you, and I love you.

Anonymous 5:

I had an imperfection on my body, which I thought was an imperfection, maybe to others not so much.
I was 14 years of age, my mother wasn't around much.

My stepfather was though.
I came to him with my concerns, and he said let me see.
Young and innocent not knowing where this would lead.
I had inverted nipples, now a normal father would go to the mother about their daughter's concerns, and my stepfather used it as a grooming tool.
He would massage my nipple until they were hard, explaining to me I had to do this and allow him to do it or they would always be inverted.
I didn't know better.
He told me not to tell my mother because she wouldn't understand.
I became 16 and told him I didn't want his help anymore.
I became ashamed.
I remember as I laid on my back and allowed my "father" to pretend to help me, I felt his private on my back.
Still to this day I am sick to my stomach.
He used my weakness and imperfections as his sick way to please himself.
I eventually told my mother, and she stayed but once they got divorce years down the

road. When we would fight she would bring it up.

I'm still in communication with my stepfather, when I did bring this up and how I felt, he told me and everyone he was just trying to help me. Now that I'm older and wiser, it didn't help.

I keep him at a distance, but my trauma is there. I try my best to release it. I was ashamed of my body for the longest. I wouldn't take my bra off with my partner. Until recently I am free with my inverted nipples. I got them pierced. Subconsciously so they wouldn't be inverted, so when my fiancé touches them I don't have flashbacks of my father.

That's my story, hopefully, this can help. Thank you.